Compl

The Prince's Youth Business Trust, of which the Prince of Wales is President, and to which royalties from this book will be donated, was established in 1986. It is a means of providing a comprehensive service to 18–25 year olds who are generally unemployed and in many cases disadvantaged, seeking to set up in business on their own account. Unlike other schemes, it is not one for job-seekers, but for job-makers. It is not aimed primarily at the most promising commercial prospects, but rather at the most deserving ones on social and humanitarian as well as economic grounds. The Trust commands the assistance of over 2,000 volunteer tutors and advisers across the country and since its inception has helped establish 4,300 businesses. Over the coming years it plans to continue to expand rapidly to meet the growing national need and to attract greater resources still.

COMPLIMENT SLIPS

compiled by
Diana Copisarow

FONTANA/Collins

First published in 1988 by Fontana Paperbacks,
8 Grafton Street, London W1X 3LA

Printed and bound in Great Britain by
William Collins Sons & Co. Ltd, Glasgow
Photoset by Rowland Phototypesetting Ltd,
Bury St Edmunds, Suffolk

Contents

FOREWORD

I am most grateful to all those many people who have contributed to this anthology for, indirectly, they have contributed to The Prince's Youth Business Trust.

Its compiler, Lady Copisarow, is very kindly donating the proceeds of this book to the Trust. Her husband was its first Chairman and the money raised will provide an annual 'Sir Alcon Copisarow Bursary' for a disabled young person.

The Trust is now helping a growing number of enterprising young people – many from areas of high unemployment – to start up their own businesses with advice from a network of professional people organised by The Prince's Youth Business Trust. I am constantly encouraged by the energy, enthusiasm and courage displayed by these young people and by the difference to their lives which can be made as a result of the seed corn finance provided by the Trust.

PREFACE

The idea for this anthology came to me quite by chance. I was feeling low after a head-hunter had dismissed my hope of finding a challenging and stimulating part-time job and my younger son endeavoured to cheer me up by enumerating my 'assets' in a verbal CV. He listed my voluntary work, my various enterprises, and my recent degree and then added 'you have four children who would like you even if you weren't their mother'.

This spontaneous and totally unintentional compliment made me reflect on others which had surprised or delighted me. I remember in Paris a Frenchman bowing low over my hand and murmuring, 'Diana, you drive like a man'!

A collection of compliments and backhanders seemed a fun way of raising money for a very worthwhile cause. When I started collecting them my husband was Chairman of The Prince's Youth Business Trust and I was greatly impressed with the enterprise and determination of the young people it helped and with the volunteers who helped them. Of course, like all successful charities it needed more money. As unemployment is a scourge which affects men and women from all backgrounds I felt I could enlist the support of well-known people from all walks of life. The response I have received has been tremendous.

The very first contribution I was sent came from Sir Robert Bellinger. It gave me great encouragement. Sir Robert offered me a quotation from Goethe:

'What you can do, or dream you can, begin it. Boldness has genius, power and magic in it.'

When I became engaged to my husband my nanny warned him, 'Diana can wheedle the hind leg off a cow'!

Whether that was ever intended as a compliment, I doubt, but it has proved a very useful attribute in this exercise! Not that I have collected all the contributions single-handed. I am indebted to a great number of friends for their free and generous help as well as to all those who have participated in this enterprise. They are too numerous to be mentioned individually, but I owe a particular debt of gratitude to three of them.

Sir Richard Dobson, who would have made a much better job of compiling an anthology than I could ever hope to do, gave me patient and wise counsel throughout. Sir James Miskin not only canvassed tirelessly on my behalf but introduced me to Ian Chapman, Chairman of Collins. To him and to all those at Collins who have been involved with this small book I am inordinately grateful. Not only have they shown me kindness, courtesy and assistance, but The Prince's Youth Business Trust will be receiving nearly three times the royalties normally paid to individual authors.

If this slim volume sells well and makes a large sum of money, its success will be largely due to David Langdon whose unmistakable illustrations will have attracted the reader initially. I asked him for help and advice and he illustrated the whole anthology. There can be no greater generosity and to him I offer my heartfelt and warmest thanks.

DIANA COPISAROW
July 1988

THE
BETTER HALF

Jeffrey Archer

At the christening of our first son, William, Professor Max Beloff was heard to say . . . 'you may pray that this child has the looks of Mary and the brains of . . . Mary'.

Brian Johnston

The housemasters' wives at Eton were pretty formidable ladies and could be a bit catty about each other. They once organized a charity concert at which each was asked to perform. One of the new wives – a recent arrival – delivered a powerful poem in French. She finished to desultory applause over which two of the 'cats' sitting in the front row were heard to say, 'Wasn't she good?' 'Yes', said the other, 'and how wise not to attempt the French accent!'

Air Chief Marshal
Sir David Evans

The choice of words in conversation is so important: especially with foreigners. Recently, this was illustrated to me very clearly when I was explaining to an overseas visitor how supportive and tolerant my wife had been throughout my long Air Force career. The actual expression that I used was that my wife was a saint. The visitor immediately replied, 'Oh, you are lucky, mine is still alive.'

Sir Alcon Copisarow

On one occasion I sought too hard to compliment my wife:
　'You're perfect!' I said.
　'Me?' she queried.
　'In fact you're pluperfect!'
　'That makes me a *had* been!' she replied.

Professor A. J. P. Taylor

Last week I had to get up early in order to join Michael Foot and Malcolm Muggeridge on a radio programme called 'Start the Week'. With both, my friendship goes back into the mists of antiquity. They were both unchanged in spirit, and even in looks. I noticed that they had both retained at its ripest the radio technique which is known in the parlance of the trade, as 'hogging the mike'. I spent most of my time silent, in a state of bemused admiration. At least, that is how it seemed to me. A highly qualified listener – my wife, of course – told me I had said quite a lot and that what I said was much more cogent than the passionate oratory of the other contenders. No wonder I like to spend so much of my days at home!
(From A.J.P. Taylor's *An Old Man's Diary*, Hamish Hamilton Ltd.)

14

'Nancy, if I were married to you . . .'

Lord King of Wartnaby

My all-time favourite Churchill quip is the retort he is said to have made to Nancy Astor's: 'Winston! You are impossible. If I were married to you I would put strychnine in your tea.' To which Winston replied: 'Nancy, if I were married to you I would drink it.'

Jean Muir

Lady Elwyn-Jones (Pearl Binder), the wife of Lord Elwyn-Jones who was Lord Chancellor at the time, said the following: 'All the wives of our ambassadors want to wear Jean Muir and I do *so* wish some of them wouldn't.'

THE FEMININE
TOUCH

Rabbi Julia Neuberger

My congregation were determined not to remark on the fact that I was female when I first started here. As a result, there was no difference in treatment, except when I became pregnant some 15 months on and they started opening occasional doors or drawing up the odd chair for me: 'You see, we didn't notice you were female until you began to bulge', said one member of the synagogue's council!

Sir John Harvey-Jones

In 1946 I was working and living with the Russians in Germany and had a friend who was a member of one of the British Women's Services. Our friendship was indeed platonic in every sense of the word and she was an absolute sweetie, but she was a very large woman of some considerable weight. She had a marvellous sense of humour and was a constant joy to be with, but was, I'm bound to admit, not exactly my beau ideal of feminine beauty.

One day, I was having a drink with one of my Russian friends and he said, 'You know, John, we like you a great deal, you could almost be a Russian. Take your taste in women for example, so strong, so sensible!'

Sir Richard Dobson

Self at dinner, to Chilean hostess:

'The Chileans did not, of course, invent women but they perfected them.'

Sir John Mills

It happened during a matinee at the Apollo Theatre where I was playing in a revival of Sir Terence Rattigan's 'Separate Tables'. The first of the two plays is a difficult one, but immensely satisfying to perform. The second is, for any emotional actor, and I hope I come into that category, a cakewalk. The construction is so perfect that the principal character grabs the sympathy of the audience with very little effort and retains it to the final curtain.

The scene I always looked forward to and enjoyed, I might even say wallowed in, was the one in which the bogus major breaks down after confessing to a rather shady past, and decides he must leave the hotel. The writing was of such high quality that I nearly always managed to produce real tears at precisely the right moment, without thinking of Mr Chips, our Yorkshire terrier, being run over in Shaftesbury Avenue, or without the aid of Dr Mackenzie's smelling salts (the actor's friend) cunningly concealed in a large handkerchief with the stopper off.

On this particular afternoon, to my delight and satisfaction, I felt a large tear trickling slowly down my cheek and, squinting down my nose to make sure that it would splash to the stage at exactly the right moment, thereby reducing my rapt and adoring audience to audible sobs and flutterings of Kleenex, I found myself looking straight at a very large lady in the front row busily knitting an even larger white sweater. I was so astonished that the tears stopped as suddenly as if they had been turned off at the main. I dried stone cold, staring at the large lady who gave me an encouraging smile and went happily on with her knitting.

I remember a party after the theatre where one actor was complaining bitterly about an audience's behaviour and lack of manners. The Master, the late Sir Noël Coward, fixed him with a beady eye and, wagging the famous forefinger, said: 'Listen dear, the theatre is a place of entertainment and people pay to be entertained, and as long as they are paying customers and not complimentaries, they are entitled to (a) yawn, (b) go to sleep, (c) snore, (d) eat pounds of chocolates from crinkly brown wrappers, (e) describe the scene taking place in a loud voice to a deaf aunt with an ear trumpet, or (f) even knit!' I have never forgotten that piece of wisdom, and I finished the performance of 'Separate Tables' while the large lady finished her white sweater without even dropping a stitch.

(From John Mills' *Up in the Clouds, Gentlemen Please* (Weidenfeld & Nicolson Ltd.)

Claire Rayner

At a party I met a man who was extremely good looking, with the most delicate features and elegant carriage. He and I discovered, during the course of our conversation, that during our schooldays we had both played Gertrude in a school production of 'Hamlet'. A mutual friend coming by at that moment – one Mel Calman, the cartoonist – was told of this remarkable shared memory and he looked from my companion's beautiful face to my much less so one and said sweetly, 'I'll bet he was more feminine in the part than you were!'

Libby Purves

When I was at university I went out with a young man called Chris Tookey – now a distinguished critic. On one occasion he put his arms around me and told me what he liked most about me was that I was built like a Volkswagen.

Dame Mary Donaldson

During the mayoralty it is customary for the Lord Mayor to be entertained by most of the livery companies. On one such occasion while sitting next to the master, I remarked on the beautiful silver possessed by that company. I leant forward, and picking up the large cup in front of the master, said, I supposed that it was better balanced than a loving cup I was given the other night and, assuming that the master's cup was still empty, I demonstrated how the loving cup had tilted forward when I had lifted it. The master watched me, in what, in retrospect, I can only assume was frozen horror as the contents, claret, cascaded over me, down my ruffles, over my badge and chain and through my dress. What, I thought to myself, is the correct protocol for a first lady Lord Mayor left sitting in a pool of claret at an all male dinner? My eye caught that of the city marshal, my esquire for the night. It was obvious to him that something was amiss, and he came to find out just what. The master appeared to be in a state of

'Built like a Volkswagen'

shock, and sat silent. I asked that the footman be sent back to the Mansion House to collect a complete change of clothing, and I swept out of the hall with as much dignity as I could muster. A striptease in the cloakroom, and a bath with paper towels removed most of the sticky wine, and within fifteen minutes I was back in my place. The majority of those present, so far as I could ascertain, were quite oblivious of my absence, or perhaps they assumed it was a new female tradition I was introducing, and all being gentlemen had just decided to turn a blind eye to my unusual behaviour.

OUT OF
THE MOUTHS
OF BABES . . .

Sir Richard Dobson

I was invited to address boys and parents at a local school prize-giving. Next day, happening to meet one of the parents, I asked him what his son's reaction had been. Answer: 'Dad, it wasn't as bad as usual.'

Sir Peter Gadsden

Dear Lord Mayor,
My name is Jane and I am six years old and I would like to have your autograph. Please could you send this to me.

Love,
Jane.

PS. Please could you send me two autographs so that I can swop one.

Each year the Lord Mayor gives a children's fancy dress party at Christmas time, when he appears in his traditional dress of Old Bailey Breeches and stock.

One of the little boys came up to me and enquired, 'Who are you?' I said I was the Lord Mayor to which he replied, 'You're not the real Lord Mayor are you?' I said that I was in fact the real Lord Mayor, to which his answer was, 'I don't believe you are the real Lord Mayor because there is Santa Claus over there, and I know he is not really Santa Claus.'

Lynne Reid-Banks

The greatest real compliment I can remember receiving was from a teacher of educationally subnormal (ESN) children in the States who told me she had never had any success with reading stories or books to her class of 12-year-olds until she read them my 'Indian in the Cupboard'. When she finished the final instalment they were all in tears, including, she said, herself, and one child said: 'Please can you make it so it goes on for ever?'

The Honourable Mr Justice Popplewell

I was at Lord's last year when a little boy, aged 9, walked up to me and said, 'Oh, Sir, can I have your autograph?' I said, 'Sonny – you don't really want my autograph.' His little face fell and he said, 'But, Sir, aren't you Nigel Popplewell's father?'

Jack Scott

Dear Mr Scott,
I have just read in my science book that a barometer forecasts the weather. If this is so, please Sir, what is your job?
Yours sincerely,
Susan . . . (aged 12).

Cliff Michelmore

Early evening, the Golden Arrow buffet at Victoria Station in the late 1950s when I was doing a nightly programme called 'Tonight' on BBC TV:

I was standing at the counter waiting to be served when I felt a slight tugging at the bottom of my jacket. Looking down there I saw looking straight back up at me a little boy, smiling.

'Are you Clifflemore?' he asked.

'Yes I am.'

'Thank you.'

I collected my coffee and was about to turn away when once more the slight tug.

'Clifflemore, this is my baby brother' and there by his side was an even smaller little boy holding up a bag.

'Have a sweetie, Clifflemore?'

What a compliment. I have long treasured the memory of those two little boys who must by now be fathers of families of their own.

Admiral of the Fleet
Sir John Fieldhouse

Returning to work, after a particularly difficult and lengthy official lunch, I got into a crowded lift in the Ministry feeling a bit conspicuous in my best uniform, aiguillettes and all. A young female messenger was next to the lift buttons and helpfully asked who wanted which floor. 'I'm six,' I said, 'Cor, aren't you big for six!' came the immediate reply, to the great amusement of the rest of us, and perhaps disconcertingly close to the truth at that moment!

'Aren't you big for six!'

LEARNING
YEARS

Michael McCrum

When I was a headmaster I once received a charming post-card. The picture was of Dartmoor Prison. The message was from a boy in the school who, alas, refrained from signing it:
   'Wish you were here!'

Sir Kenneth Berrill

A chronically lazy student of mine had achieved very poor results in his end-of-year examinations and I was having an embarrassing time putting to him the likely reasons for this disappointing outcome. Taking pity on me and trying to be helpful, the student interjected: 'Don't worry too much about it, Sir. I expect the fault is as much mine as it is yours.'

Professor Sir Karl Popper

In October 1946, in R. B. Braithwaite's room in King's College, Cambridge, Karl Popper read a paper, deliberately hoping to provoke Wittgenstein into defending his view that there are no philosophical problems. He succeeded in doing so and after a very lively exchange and angered by Popper's seemingly light-hearted treatment of the matter Wittgenstein stormed out of the room.

'Wish you were here'

'After Wittgenstein left us we had a very pleasant discussion, in which Bertrand Russell was one of the main speakers. And Braithwaite afterwards paid me a compliment (perhaps a doubtful compliment) by saying that I was the only man who has managed to interrupt Wittgenstein in the way in which Wittgenstein interrupted everyone else.

'Next day in the train to London there were, in my compartment, two students sitting opposite each other, a boy reading a book and a girl reading a leftish journal. Suddenly she asked: "Who is this man Karl Popper?" He replied: "Never heard of him." Such is fame.'

(From Professor Sir Karl Popper's autobiographical work *Unended Quest*, Flamingo)

Frederic Raphael

It would require a rare imagination to devise a supreme compliment which contained, as its key ingredient, the word 'aviator'. However, it was central to one of the most significant tributes offered by one genius of the twentieth century to another. It happened, as I recall, like this.

Ludwig Wittgenstein, who had known Bertrand Russell before the First World War, was uncertain of whether or not he should return to philosophy after it. He therefore sent his new work, which was, more or less, what would later be known as the *Tractatus Logico-Philosophicus*, to Russell. He asked the older man to read it and to report, without tact, on its merits. As Russell later told the story, Wittgenstein told him that if his work lacked merit, he would abandon philosophy for good and become a pilot. (The Wittgenstein family was deeply involved in technology and Wittgenstein himself was a practical man who designed a famous house for, I believe, his sister.) Russell read the *Tractatus* and was made aware of arguments implicit in it which, in due course, would lead him to give up all hope of doing breakthrough work in the theory of mathematics. One could imagine a lesser man (and perhaps a greater one) wanting to do nothing more than to discourage a young rival who, in a way which only a great mind could see, was going to be greater than his master. Russell tells us, with juicy dryness, that having considered the text, he told Wittgenstein that he should 'on no account become an aviator'.

A. S. Byatt

The compliment I think of most often and with most surprise is one from Sir Randolph Quirk when he was Professor of English at University College, and I was weeping in his office about a (very real) tragedy. 'Do you know, Antonia,' he said, in a disinterested and intellectually anxious voice, 'that when you are very distressed you speak in complete sentences?' This counters all the conventional wisdom about spoken English structures I meet on my Committee of Inquiry into the teaching of English Language, and pleases me (and comforted me) for some reason.

Professor Sir Randolph Quirk

I never thought I would be analogously honoured, but not long ago, on opening a book from a distant land, I was gratified to read in the Preface:

Many scholars in London and Oxford were generous with patient and expert advice during my researches, and to the eminent Professor Randolph Quirk I am not in the least indebted.

Lieutenant-General
Sir Peter Hudson

An Etonian friend of mine gained a report at the end of one half from his mathematics master which described him as: 'Gloomily incompetent'.

Sir Jeremy Morse

I was introduced at Oxford to an Indian academic called Dr Biswas. Having recently enjoyed V. S. Naipaul's novel I immediately said, 'Oh! "A House for Mr Biswas",' and then wished I hadn't, remembering how a number of my English acquaintances disliked sharing their name with well-known characters in fact or fiction. I need not have worried. With a sweet smile he replied: 'Biswas is quite a common name in India, but Mr Naipaul has made it immortal.'

Professor Sir Fred Hoyle

When I was a research student (1936–39), we students at Cambridge were given to a measure of subtlety in the way we treated each others' opinions. I found to my amusement that the whole gamut from high praise to extreme denigration could be conveyed in only three words, of which there were six variants. Going from praise to denigration from one to six, the list has a pleasing and remarkable symmetry about it:

No: 1 – Right every time.
No: 2 – Wrong for once.
No: 3 – Right this time.
No: 4 – Wrong this time.
No: 5 – Right for once.
No: 6 – Wrong every time.

The slight subtlety comes in realizing that 2 is better than 3, and that 5 is worse than 4.

SIMPLY DIVINE

Father Michael Hollings

As Chaplain to Roman Catholics at Oxford University, I was in my room one day when a young man, an undergraduate student, who had just got a first class degree, came in to see me. He was very worried about an equally brilliant friend of his whom he thought had lost faith in the Roman Catholic Church of God.

Paul said to me he wanted to help his friend – what could he do? We thought of various things – and finally I suggested he might get his friend to come to have a chat.

He went off and came back a couple of days later, crestfallen. He said he had talked to his friend who refused to come to see me. His friend had said, 'No! It would be a waste of time. I should only hear the same old arguments – and anyhow, why should I go to talk to someone who only has a quarter of my intelligence?'

The Most Reverend
Derek Worlock

Some years ago I was accompanying, as his chaplain, an elderly Cardinal Archbishop who was making an official visit to a Mediterranean island community. Unfortunately he was taken ill and I was asked to deputize for him at a reception given in his honour. The organizers rushed me into a crowded hall where many excited persons were waiting. The situation was explained to the local chairman of the organization, and some of my background was mentioned.

He went to the microphone to address his members who had gathered in such great number. 'For many weeks,' he said, 'we have prepared ourselves for the visit of the Most Eminent Cardinal Archbishop of London. Now we hear he is indisposed. He has sent in his place a distinguished cleric who, it seems, is a well-known television personality.' There was a buzz of excitement, which was hushed as he turned to me and asked loudly and pointedly: '*What* did you say your name is?'

Lord Quinton

A Carmelite friar on P. G. Wodehouse, when asked to say a Mass to his memory (1975-ish).

'Well, I will, since you ask me. But in the case of someone who brought such joy to so many people in the course of his life, do you really think it's necessary?'

The Right Reverend William Westwood

I was once described by both the *Eastern Daily Press* and the *Sunday Times* as the 'human face of the Church', but my pride at this compliment was tempered by the introduction offered by the Bishop of Ely: 'This is the Bishop of Peterborough. You can take him anywhere but you can't leave him.'

Rabbi Lionel Blue

I always remember this backhander: an elderly lady came up to me after a talk and said: 'I really liked your talk; you sounded so sincere this week'.

Lord King of Wartnaby

A Yorkshire friend of mine told me of what he thinks was a compliment. He had known the local Catholic priest for many years. They bumped into each other one day as the priest was calling on some of the families in the village. After the usual greetings the priest remarked with a slight shake of the head: 'You are not a member of the faith, are you Mr K—.' 'No, Father.' 'Ah well,' reflected the priest, 'if you keep your bowels regular and say your prayers, you'll not be coming to much harm.'

MUSIC
TO THE EARS

Simon Rattle

Of all the many strange and confusing compliments I have received, the following from an enormously over-enthusiastic lady sticks in the mind: 'Oh, Mr Rattle, your orchestra is just so wonderful, did you know I could hear each of your violinists separately?'

Sir Georg Solti

In 1945/55 I conducted a series of performances of Mozart's 'Marriage of Figaro' at the Lyric Opera in Chicago. The chief music critic in the city at that time was a formidable lady called Claudia Cassidy, whose influence on subsequent Chicago music life was quite considerable, to say the least . . . I have good reason to remember her review of the first night of that production, which contained words along the following lines:

'Solti smiled happily throughout the big ensembles of the opera; he would have done better to cut his throat . . .'

Sir Yehudi Menuhin

Some time ago, finding myself stranded in Portland Place, and with my usual optimism not imagining I would meet

'Better to have cut his throat'

with any difficulty in finding a cab to take me back to my then house in Highgate Village, I confidently flagged down the first one that came by in that elegant street. To my hurt surprise, on hearing of my hoped-for destination, a look of extreme distaste soured the driver's face as though I had asked him to take me to a leper colony: 'Naoh!' he said, 'Too far by 'alf', and shot off.

No one had told me that in order to lay claim to be transported anywhere one might reasonably or unreasonably wish, the trick was to put one foot firmly through the open door, and thus installing oneself irrevocably, demand to be driven to John O'Groats.

With diminishing ardour and diminishing hope, I flagged several more, semaphoring wildly, all to no effect as these Lords of Transport swept by, indomitable and merciless profiles showing their lack of interest in this sadly flapping creature.

At last one cab came that actually stopped. However, when I – by now tentatively – mentioned Highgate Village, he too shook an alienated head, shoved in the clutch and, as he drove off shouted: 'And has anyone ever told you how much *shorter* you look offstage?'

Nonetheless, that slap in the face was fully compensated by another driver who not only accepted me willingly, albeit I explained that I had as usual not a penny on me, but on that long trip northwards engaged me with the talk of his daughter's playing the oboe and the whole family's love of music, so enchanting me that I took his name and address and invited them all to my next concert, which happened to be a few days later.

On arrival home I begged him to wait while I ran into the house to get money from that bottomless source, our house-keeper Millie (known as Millie Rothschild, the Banker). He prevented me, saying that it had been his pleasure and enjoyment and that even had I not offered him the concert seats, he had determined from the outstart not to charge me.

My confidence in the courtesy of most taxi-drivers was thus fully restored.

Rabbi Hugo Gryn

A wealthy man in a provincial town decided to study the violin. He engaged the Professor of Violin at the local conservatory and, after a few months of lessons, informed his teacher that he had hired the auditorium for his first public performance.

The teacher was appalled; pleaded for more time, but invitations had been sent out and, to make the best of it, the teacher offered, 'I had better accompany you myself and find an easy programme'.

Came the great evening and, on the way to the stage, the Professor asked his colleague, the Professor of Piano, to help with the turning of pages. Eventually the recital took place.

The following day this review appeared in the local press: '. . . the gentleman who turned the pages should, of course, have played the piano, and the gentleman at the piano should have played the violin. The gentleman who played the violin, may in a few years, qualify to turn the pages . . .'.

Sir Neville Marriner

One of the first prizes the Academy of St Martin-in-the-Fields won was the Edison Award, then presented yearly, with much pomp, in Amsterdam. There were many classes of awards for all kinds of music and the winners were invited for two days to the ceremony, a gala concert and parties.

The second time the Academy won, we were asked to give the concert, an honour and an ordeal, considering the number of our peers in the audience. That year, Gustave Leonhardt, the distinguished harpsichord player, was also a prizewinner, and the authorities requested we play Bach's Fifth Brandenburg Concerto together. During the rehearsal I was much in awe of this elegant and renowned musician.

The concert opened with a Handel Concerto Grosso, and as I stood at the top of the formidable downward flight of stairs which is the only way onto the platform of the Concertgebouw, Leonhardt was waiting there, peacefully, for his piece to come. Taking a look at my nervous face, he patted me on the back, giving me a gentle push to start me down the steps and saying, 'Play as you've never played before – play well.'

Sir Richard Dobson

Noel Annan, when he was Provost of King's, used to conduct the college orchestra on Sunday evenings. One Sunday a very distinguished professional conductor was invited to the concert and asked what he thought of the Provost's conducting. The great man replied, 'I think he keeps time very well with the music.'

TV TIMES

Lynne Reid-Banks

When my first play, 'It Never Rains . . .' was given an airing on BBC TV in the 'fifties, a *friend* of mine who was finding his feet in television criticism on the *Evening Standard* (I think it was), rang me the morning after. 'Lynne, I've got *the most marvellous* line for my review of your play! No, listen, you're going to *love* it, it's great, I thought of it in the night . . . wait for it now! Ready? "It never rains . . . *but it bores!*" '

Robert Powell

From a letter sent to the Director General of Yorkshire TV

Dear Sir,

I am writing to you on behalf of Robert Powell. He is a splendid actor and I enjoyed his playing Hannibal. Also his readings in the Word of Good Friday. However, nothing to my mind surpasses his depiction of Jesus of Nazareth. He was superb. However, I cannot help but feel concerned for him, because after watching Jesus of Nazareth I became aware of a change in Robert Powell that I fealt (*sic*) had nothing to do with make up. He looks to me like a man under stress and I do sincerely hope that he is not being pushed too far. He is too much of an asset to lose and I hope that someone will see their way clear to getting him to take a holiday.

Mike Yarwood

Robin Day once said to me, 'I don't mind you impersonating me, but I do object to you getting more money for being me, than I do!'

Sir Robin Day

In the late 'fifties, during my early period as an ITN newscaster, my illusions about the impact of high-powered newscasting were healthily shattered. During a period of grim and depressing news, a charming middle-aged lady came up to me one day on the Underground and said: 'Mr Day, I so like the way you do your news. You don't look as though you believe a word of it.'

From time to time I have had a healthy reminder that not everyone gazing at the little box has been mesmerized by my words of wisdom or by the film which has gone with them. I recall one ITN news. It was a big night for news. I felt pleased with the bulletin. It was full of vivid film, which gave one an extra zest in introducing it.

I gave an eye-witness report of the afternoon's Commons debate, having sweated blood to compress three hours' argument into a lucid, graphic ninety-five seconds. Then a brisk, incisive studio interview, bringing out all the essential points in two and a quarter minutes. Then a 'hot' last-minute item, telephoned through to the studio by the subeditor was ad-libbed on to the earlier version of the story. Finally, a flash of spontaneous wit, on which much labour had been spent.

Was it not a programme to be proud of? I went downstairs to the newsroom. The telephone rang. Congratulations from the editor? Loving compliments from a girl-friend? A protest from a politician? 'It's for you,' said the chief sub, 'a viewer in Croydon says to tell Robin Day to get his hair cut.'

ARMY DAYS

Lieutenant-General
Sir Peter Hudson

I was in command of the only Brigade in Northern Ireland when the present 'troubles' started. After two years I left and my Brigade Major, himself an Irishman said, 'Well Brigadier, it's been tough and I can't say its been much fun – but we've had a lot of laughs.'

Sir David Hunt

In 1965 I was appointed High Commissioner in Cyprus. There were living in the island then, as now, a number of people who had retired from the services. One of them, a former regular officer who left the army with the rank of major, was heard loudly declaiming at a cocktail party a month or so after my arrival: 'This man Hunt is just the sort of man we want. Poor old — (my predecessor) was no good at all; far too honest and straightforward.'

Sir James Spicer MP

An official visit to the Devon and Dorset Regiment in Berlin was to be followed by a meeting of Centre and Centre Right

Parliamentarians. At the very last minute, Sir William Clark, a very senior Member of Parliament, agreed to join me.

A telephone call to the Devon and Dorsets made by me confirmed that we would be met on arrival and that Sir William would be with me. All went well, and the arrangements on our arrival in Berlin were quite splendid. However, I sensed a slightly dismissive approach to Sir William Clark. Much the same attitude was apparent at lunch in the Officers' Mess. Finally, a rather embarrassed Commanding Officer explained to me that the message passed to him from me had read, 'Jim Spicer rang to confirm his arrival time. He will be accompanied by his civilian clerk!'

John Julius Norwich

From the report of an Officers' Training College on a friend of mine. The Commanding Officer's summing-up consisted of a single sentence: 'Any soldier who follows this officer will do so only out of curiosity.'

Sir Christopher Leaver

I was in the army, newly posted as Junior Subaltern to my regiment, and upon my first Regimental Mess night the drink flowed freely. No officer was permitted to leave the party before the Commanding Officer. At around 5 a.m., exceedingly drunk, he decided to go home and staggered out. Although I had enjoyed the evening greatly I was several degrees more sober than he and, thinking it was my duty to

'Only out of curiosity . . .'

be helpful, I followed and asked him if he would like me to drive him to his house. This normally delightful and placid man turned on me, scarlet in the face, saying, 'I suppose you think I'm drunk and incapable', and with that ripped the entire driving seat from his pre-war Morris 8 and hurled it at me. I then watched him sitting on the floor boards driving himself home.

The following morning I was summoned by the Adjutant to report to the CO and I feared the worst. 'Do you know', he opened, 'you have been here only months and already you are the most popular officer in the Regiment', and then raising his voice shouted, 'And that's why you are the worst!' As I saluted and turned about to leave he added very quietly, 'Thank you for the offer – I should have let you drive me.'

ACROSS THE ATLANTIC

Sir Charles Villiers

We often holiday with American friends and their humour delights us. For example:

A Brooklyn boy, staying with friends in Long Island said: 'Dad's a boid.'

'No', said his friend, 'that's a bird.'

'Well,' said t'other, 'it choips like a boid.'

President Truman liked to jog along the banks of the Potomac. One day he slipped and fell in the river. Three boys who were fishing pulled him out. The President was shaken but grateful and asked the boys what he could do for them. The first and second boys asked for commissions in the Army and Navy, but the third hung his head and would not reply. The President pressed him and the boy said:

'Mr President, I would like a military funeral.'

The President said, 'Why the hell?'

'Well', said the boy, 'that's what I'll need when I tell my family what I have done this morning.'

Sir Richard Dobson

Seeing a young family struggling up the steps at Richmond station, I gave them a hand with their baggage. When we got to the top, the young man said, 'Thank you, Sir, you are a gentleman.' I was touched because that definition is not current in this country except in the context of public speeches or public lavatories. As he spoke, I realized the chap was an American!

Sir Hugh Casson

The only 'put down' I can remember was from Mrs Palmer the famous Chicago hostess 1890ish, to a Fifth Avenue show-off who said (showing her his house), 'This is my Louis XIV drawing room . . .' 'Indeed', said Mrs Palmer, 'what makes you think so?'

Sam Wanamaker

From a passing American in a New York street: 'You were terrific in "Viva Zapata"!' I thanked him of course. I could not face telling him I was not in the picture. Why spoil his pleasure of recognition.

Another American in Berlin, or Rome, or some place: 'I am one of your greatest fans! I love your work – but would you mind telling me your name?'

Brian Clark

A few years ago I was commissioned to write a ten-minute play entitled *America* for production at the Louisville Festival of Modern American Drama. There were to be nine other such plays by non-American playwrights and the idea was to provide a view of America through foreign eyes.

I decided to write about American foreign policy in the form of the afternoon soap operas on Network TV. These are full of tense and traumatic confrontations between men and women who have betrayed, hurt and misled each other in every way possible. They are all unbelievably cliché ridden and overlaid with soupy electronic organ music. I chose three couples representing America with Vietnam, Central America, and the Middle East and sat for one week in a New York hotel noting every cliché that limped from the loudspeaker. I managed to write a play with three couples from three soaps and called it 'Switching in the Afternoon', and every single line was an actual cliché from a soap opera.

The audience seemed to see the joke and enjoy it. Not so the critic of the *Observer*, Robert Cushman. After dealing with several of the other plays by Fugard, Friel and so on he came to mine.

'Clark's play was terrible. It was full of clichés.'

Norman Willis

At a dinner in the White House honouring Nobel Prize winners of the western hemisphere, J. F. Kennedy said:

'I want to tell you how welcome you all are to the White House. I think this is the most extraordinary collection of talent, of human knowledge, that has ever been gathered together at the White House, with the possible exception of when Thomas Jefferson dined alone.'

A TASTE OF
THE ORIENT

Lord MacLehose of Beoch

Sir Murray,

In retrospection of the honour Your Excellency have bestowed upon me in our meeting which has lasted over half an hour in spite of your considerable pressure of official matters. No doubt, my personal appreciation of Your Excellency's greatness and kindness will, forever, be vivid in memory.

During our conversation, I have been impressed that Your Excellency are a magnetic personality possessing the wisdom of Solomon, the understanding of Lincoln and strategy of Churchill. You have incomparable enthusiasm for my present situation with sentimental consolation that has topsy-turvy survived my dying spirit. Now, I must stand up again to realize my commitments for serving the community in the near future.

Hoping that I shall have the opportunity to renew your acquaintance,

Yours most respectfully.

Sir John Grenside

I recall many years ago being engaged in negotiations with some high-ranking Japanese businessmen, one of whose most frequent ploys was to preface their more outrageous half-truths with 'very frankly speaking'.

After a protracted session lasting long into the evening had ended with solemn nodding of heads and an apparent meeting of minds, I was greeted the following morning with the opening gambit: 'Very frankly speaking, having reflected on what you suggested last night, we have concluded there must have been some misunderstanding for we are sure no gentleman would have proposed what our notes indicate you may think we have agreed.'

Rabbi Hugo Gryn

The lecture in Japan was to last an hour and, as the audience included no English speakers, a translator was to be duly engaged.

After the first 15 minutes the lecturer paused and the translator stepped up to the microphone, said half a dozen words and sat down. Puzzled, the lecturer went on. Fifteen minutes later he stopped again, and again half a dozen words from the translator. And so, after forty-five minutes, again. At the end, the translator came forward, uttered four words, gave a small bow.

The audience applauded politely before breaking for tea and sake.

The lecturer, more puzzled than ever, found his own English-speaking colleague, and asked him to explain: 'As a matter of fact, I kept a verbatim record of what was said in Japanese', said his friend. 'The first intervention was, "So far he has said nothing new." Then he told us, "I don't think he *will* say anything new." And at the end he said, "I was absolutely right".'

Sir Peter Reynolds

An old friend arrived some years ago in Iran as the new Managing Director. To his dismay he found the main factory was about to go on strike and, in true Empire fashion, he felt he should address the people. He mugged up some Iranian and ended his speech by saying, 'We must go hand in hand into the future together.' To his amazement this was greeted with loud and delighted laughter. He had actually said, 'We must go hand in hand into the bath together.' There was no strike.

AFTER DINNER

His Honour Judge
Sir James Miskin

On starting my appointment as Recorder of London I attended my first lunch at the Old Bailey where the Sheriffs were our hosts and all the Judges were present along with some other guests: an old friend rose to say grace: he fixed me with a beady eye and said, 'Oh God, may we ever remain needful of the minds of others,' and it was not a mistake.

A few days later the *Wimbledon News* published an article about a case I had finished and its headline read, 'Mr James Miskin Esq., W.C., Recorder of London'. A friend suggested that they must have thought I was a Writer to the Signet but could not spell.

At dinner that night with a City Livery Company I noticed on their menu both their crest and motto which was 'Semper modus fidelis', 'thank God the *Wimbledon News* is not here,' I thought to myself, 'they would at once attribute to me the motto "semper commodus fidelis".'

A week later I lunched with the Court of Aldermen: a senior past Lord Mayor rose and proposed my health: it was at the height of the rabbit crisis centring on myxomatosis: he included the words 'we must of course all pray that we have not been sentenced to an indeterminate sentence of Miskimatosis'.

Sir Peter Reynolds

Some years ago our Chief Scientist led a delegation to Russia. At the final dinner, having learnt two words of Russian by careful observation, he opened his speech in Russian – to shocked silence from his interpreter and guests. Instead of 'Ladies and Gentlemen', he had opened with 'Latrines and Water Closets'.

Sir Isaiah Berlin

There was a man to whom a testimonial dinner was given. After all the speeches about his merits had been made, he rose to his feet and said something of this kind: 'I deeply appreciate the wonderful compliments which have been paid me and the descriptions of my life and my work, which I found entirely appropriate and accurate, and for which, therefore, I am naturally grateful. There is only one of my attributes which nobody has mentioned, and that is my exceptional modesty.'

Sir David Hunt

A club in Sussex, where I live, asked me to speak after dinner. The chairman wound up his introductory remarks as follows: 'Now some of you here tonight have heard Sir David Hunt speak before and some of you haven't. Those who haven't will be looking forward to a thoroughly entertaining address.'

Sir Randolph Quirk

A friend is fond of reporting how she was presented by a bumbling chairman with the words:

'Ladies and gentlemen. It is my privilege to introduce this evening a speaker who despite her very busy life was kind enough to respond favourably to our invitation. We would, of course have been content to have a less distinguished lecturer, but we couldn't find one.'

Lord Cledwyn of Penrhos

Some years ago I was in North Wales sharing a platform in support of a worthy cause with the late Hugh Griffith, the well-known actor. I made my speech but Hugh was late arriving and, after he sat down, the Chairman rose to welcome him with the following words:

'Ladies and gentlemen, we have now arrived at the anticlimax of our meeting and it gives me pleasure to call upon Mr Hugh Griffith to address you.'

Lloyd George used to tell the following story against himself.

During the great controversy about disestablishment in Wales, the Bishop of St Asaph, Dr Edwards, addressed a very successful meeting in Bangor against disestablishment. The local pro-disestablishment committee met the following day and decided to invite Lloyd George to address a meeting in support of the cause as its most eloquent advocate. When the time came the hall was once again full and the Chairman got up to introduce the speaker. 'Ladies and gentlemen,' he said, 'a month ago a meeting against disestablishment was addressed by the Bishop of St Asaph, the biggest rogue in Christendom but,' he said, pointing at Lloyd George, 'thank God we've got his match here tonight.'

Sir Richard Dobson

I used to think it such a pity,
when I was young and they were old,that, though my words
were wise and witty,
they left my audiences cold.

Then, when I was anointed King,
all of a sudden all was smiles;
bad jokes, old stories, anything –
I had them rolling in the aisles.

Now once again my quips fall flat
for I am old and they are young;
I'm forced to the conclusion that
henceforth I'd better hold my tongue.

(*Envoi*, composed for a farewell dinner)

PERSONAL
APPEARANCES

Bryan Forbes and
Nanette Newman

In my more youthful days when I was purely a stage actor, I once received a fan letter from a man whose credentials were doubtless dubious, who stated that although he admired my performance, what he admired most were the trousers I wore in the third act and would I send them to him when the play finished. I have never been able to work that one out.

My wife Nanette (Newman), who appears regularly on television, faces different hazards, for it is curious that whereas people known only for stage and screen appearances seldom, if ever, come into direct contact with their audiences, the moment you appear on television, viewers immediately regard you as part of the family. I suppose the simple reason for this is that you enter into their homes and they come to believe that you are an intimate. This presents its own problems and Nanette and I have often laughed about an occasion when we were both doing a charity performance in Bath. Nanette went out on an errand to secure some props at the last moment. It was pouring with rain and she was immediately drenched. While making the purchase she was approached by a middle-aged couple who circled her for two or three minutes until the man remarked audibly to his wife, 'Yes, it is. It is her. It is Nanette Newman.' Whereupon the woman thrust her face very close to Nanette's and looking her straight in the eye said, 'Oh dear, doesn't she look bedraggled.'

David Jacobs

It was just before midnight at the Festival Hall many years ago, I was to introduce the star of the evening, Frank Sinatra. The audience, including HRH Princess Margaret, was eagerly awaiting his arrival on stage. Having worked with him before but not having met him on that day, I knocked on his dressing room door which was opened by his black valet, George Jacobs. When I introduced myself he said, with a big smile on his face, 'Do you think we could be related?'

Mr Sinatra was sitting in an armchair wearing only a dress shirt, bow-tie, underpants and black silk socks. We chatted for a while and when the time came for him to dress he climbed onto a table so that George Jacobs could hold his unfolded trousers and he, Mr Sinatra, could put one stiff leg in after the other. Mr Jacobs zipped up Mr Sinatra's flies and lifted him off the table. His feet slipped into his patent leather shoes, his jacket was produced into which he put two stiff arms. We then walked together to the side of the stage, Mr Sinatra's gait resembling that of a penguin. 'Why', I asked him, 'do you put your clothes on in such a strange fashion and walk in that way?' To which he replied, 'I know my voice is in good order but when I get out onto the stage I don't want to be wearing a crumpled suit like yours.'

Robert Powell

One comment I can remember well was from a review of a television play from the 60s: 'Robert Powell, with a face like a haunted parking meter . . .'

'A crumpled suit like yours'

Richard Briers

W. A. Darlington, the critic of the *Daily Telegraph* described me playing Hamlet like a demented typewriter, and Noël Coward said I was the greatest Farceur he had seen, because I never ever hung about!

Humphrey Lyttleton

The neatest compliment ever paid to me was from Peter Black, erstwhile TV critic on the *Daily Mail*, whom I first knew when I was a cartoonist on the same paper. Later I appeared on TV with my band, and in his review, Peter wrote: 'Humphrey Lyttleton has smartened himself up. He now looks as if he has just climbed out of a haystack. In his *Daily Mail* days, he contrived to look as if he had brought the haystack with him.'

'Just climbed out of a haystack . . .'

THE REAL THING

Cleo Laine

Here's a compliment I've had a couple of times – I'm never sure how to take it. It goes something like this:

Bump into fan, who is very surprised even to see me, shopping alone. Once over the shock, the comment is, 'Why, you look much nicer than on the tele!'

The Right Honourable Lord Prior

I was addressing a meeting in Ted Heath's constituency in Bexley and was constantly interrupted and heckled by a lady in the front row. After the meeting was over, I went to speak to her. Before I could get a word out, she said to me, 'At any rate you are not so bad looking as you are on TV. On TV you are bloody 'orrible!'

George Melly

I remember being very pleased when an attractive young woman journalist turned up to interview me and said when I opened the door, 'Oh, I was expecting a much older man.'

Mary Whitehouse

Coming back home from London by train one day, I noticed that the only other person in the carriage kept looking at me most intently and every time I glanced up she looked away! This seemed to go on pretty well for the whole journey until I stood up to get out at Colchester.

As I did so she said, most apologetically, 'You must have thought me very rude staring at you like that but I kept wondering if you were Mrs Whitehouse. But now I can see you properly I realize you're much better looking!'

'Well, that's a relief anyway,' I said, keeping my face perfectly straight until the train had taken my companion on her journey. Then I had a bit of a giggle to myself and told the story with great relish when I arrived home!

'You're much better looking!'

MISTAKEN IDENTITY

Hayley Mills

This is a little incident that happened when I was 13 years old and in Hollywood for the first time, making 'Polyanna' for Walt Disney.

I was lying around the pool at the Beverly Wiltshire Hotel reeking of Ambre Solaire, which is *de rigueur* over there, when a girl came up to me and thrust a piece of paper and a biro into my face and asked for my autograph. I leapt greasily to my feet and obliged with alacrity; it being the first autograph I had ever been asked to give. After having written a novel I handed the paper and pen back to her, whereupon she read it and looked up at me with a look of singular surprise and disappointment on her face and said, 'Oh dear, I thought you were Sue Lyon.' . . . Collapse of stout party.

Ernie Wise

I once had dinner with David Coleman, the famous sports commentator.

Over coffee, I said to him, 'The papers have been criticizing you over getting names wrong when you are reporting sport.' David was most indignant, he said, 'I never make mistakes with names, Eric.'

Arnold Wesker

Around 1962 I was visiting the studio of the painter Felix Topolski who had just completed the designs and drawings for the new hotel in Sloane Street. Visiting him at the same time was the American property man who'd built the hotel. Rather stereotype I'm afraid: corpulent, badly dressed and cigar smoking. Topolski introduced us. Being Polish he did so with Slavic lavishness. I cannot remember what he said of the property tycoon but to him of me he said: 'And this is Arnold Wesker, England's leading young playwright!' The corpulent American took out his cigar, looked me up and down and said: 'Well, if you're England's leading young playwright why isn't your name John Osborne?'

Raymond Baxter

Like it or not, it is a product of regular appearances on television that one is recognized by total strangers. Personally I have always taken this as a compliment, but I have been told by some that they resent it bitterly. As a professional broadcaster throughout my working life, my view is that the time to be bothered is when one is *not* recognized. But certainly, my own experience has been more of pleasure than annoyance.

Of course it is not merely a question of recognition. It is the response to that recognition which matters. This can vary from a cheery, 'Ulloa Raymond mate. Ain't seen you on the box lately', to 'Oh, excuse me, Mr Baxter, but you've been in our sitting-room so often that I feel I know you.'

But where the real fun lies is in those cases of half-recognition, or best of all, mistaken identity. "Ere Mabel. That's 'im. 'Im on the tele. Oh you know. Old Whatsisname who reads the news', or 'That's the bloke what does Tomorrow's World.' I still hear that long years after my departure from that programme.

My daughter has followed me through a street market deliberately to eavesdrop on the observations of those passing in the opposite direction. Our all-time high was when I was mistaken for Peter Finch, but I have obligingly signed many an autograph as Richard Baker, James Burke or Brian Johnston, according to whoever I may have been mistaken for at the time. After all, we are all in the same business so why disappoint a customer?

Some years ago at one of the rare Awards Ceremonies to which I have been invited, I met Les Dawson for the first time. 'I think it's marvellous' he wheezed, 'the way you explain all that complicated technical and scientific stuff.' 'Oh rubbish', I replied modestly. 'I know it is', he said, 'but you do it beautifully!'

Probably the most confused compliment I have ever received was contained in a viewer's letter. 'I do so admire' it read, 'your ability in presenting your programme. And I think your impersonation of Barbra Streisand is out of this world.' I didn't know whether to sign my letter of thanks Raymond or Stanley!

Baroness Blackstone

I was on a train with my son, then aged 18, who struck up a conversation with some young men in the next seats. It was about music. To illustrate their discussion they turned on a large 'boogie box' to listen to a tape of rock music. I frowned and looked irritated. One of the young men looked at me and said to my son, 'Your sister thinks we should turn it off.'

John le Carré

A friend of mine, male, was approached at a party by a notorious homosexual, who peered at him as if in half-recognition, before asking, 'Excuse me. Have I *had* you?' My friend, who was rather pompous, let out an appalled, 'Certainly not!' and received a pat. And a reassuring reply: 'Never mind, dear. It's nice to be fancied'.

John Bratby

Brian Walden, looking at my portrait of him said, 'I'll have that one. Do another portrait of me and I'll have that.'

Lord Kindersley

While on tour as chairman of the Commonwealth Development Corporation with one of my directors, HRH The Prince of Wales, I was leading the way when we arrived at the house of one of our general managers on a farming project in deepest Africa. Although I had visited the project only 12 months before, the general manager's wife curtsied to me and welcomed me as the Royal guest!

Dulcie Gray

One evening in the 40s, my husband Michael Denison and I were invited to the London film première of 'The Years Between' starring Valerie Hobson and Michael Redgrave. I was just beginning my film career, and had a small part in the film, although I was, in fact, under contract to Sir Alexander Korda by this time. Michael had only just been released from the army, and was finding my new life a little bewildering. Suddenly a man appeared out of the crowd, came straight towards me, bowed low over my hand, kissed it, and said urgently, 'I have all your affairs in order so that you can leave the country immediately'. He gave me a conspiratorial smile, and left me.

Both of us bowed graciously to his retreating back, and Michael was astounded, 'What on earth was all that about?' he asked.

'I suppose it was the Income Tax man getting things ready for a new film,' I said vaguely.

'No. No, surely it was Sir Alexander Korda?' said Michael.

But it later transpired that it was a travel agent who thought he had been talking to Googie Withers.

Sir Brian Rix

Rotary had asked me to present the raffle prizes after a show and the man who did the asking was our vet, then treating Bastien for a particularly lovely condition known as wet eczema. Anyway, he assured me that we would be met at the door (of Wandsworth Town Hall) and all would be well.

Unfortunately he omitted to tell the doorman about these arrangements and also omitted to have anyone awaiting our arrival. The doorman did *not* recognise us.

'Where's your tickets?'

'We have no tickets. We are guests, here to present the raffle prizes.'

'We get bleeding try-ons like that, mate, every night of the week. No ticket, no entrance.'

'Look, I'm Brian Rix and this is my wife Elspet Gray. You must have seen us on the box.'

'How can I watch the bleeding box when I'm 'ere every bleeding night?'

We were about to leave when a flustered Rotarian ran up and whisked us past the glowering doorman and, with profuse apologies, ushered two tight-lipped Rixes into the hall and to a table peopled by our local MP Sir Hugh Linstead, Evelyn Laye and her husband Frank Lawton. To cover our confusion Elspet turned to talk to Sir Hugh. Unfortunately *her* confusion was such that she mistook our MP for our vet.

'Bastien is so much better since you gave him those pills,' she trilled. 'All that nasty weeping has stopped but he still looks a trifle poxy.' Sir Hugh was, to say the least, non-plussed. Under the table I kicked Elspet, who suddenly realized her *faux pas* and you could see the blush spreading upwards from her toes. By the time it reached the roots of her red hair I had grabbed her and was treading the light fantastic. Sir Hugh stayed, open-mouthed, at the table wondering, no doubt, if all actresses were as scatty. After that Elspet always voted for Sir Hugh, even though she is, at heart, a Liberal. What you might call a poxy vote.

(From *My Farce from my Elbow*, reprinted by permission of Martin Secker and Warburg Ltd)

AMBIGUITIES

The Right Honourable Lord Elwyn-Jones

I was briefed some years ago to appear in a political case in Tripoli, Libya. This was in the time of King Idris. When I arrived there and informed the Ministry of Justice of my wish to take part in the proceedings, for the defence, I was told the following day that they had to adjourn the trial until the following week. This was a device I had met previously in seeking to help in human rights cases.

Unfortunately, I knew I had undertaken to defend in a murder trial at Cardiff Assizes in the following week and I was not sure of the date. I therefore cabled my clerk in the Temple asking him to inform me of the date of the Cardiff murder trial. The next day I received a telephone call from our Embassy in Tripoli asking: 'What on earth is going on? A cable for you has been intercepted by Libyan security and it reads "Cable received. Murder fixed for Wednesday".' The caller went on to say that the police were on their way to my hotel to investigate the matter. However, when I explained the circumstances, our Embassy undertook to explain the position to the police, which they did successfully. I was accordingly saved from a long period of incarceration in Libya.

Professor Sir Alfred Ayer

More than fifty years ago I was invited to dine at his home by Charles Morgan, the dramatic critic of *The Times*, and a successful novelist. We had never met before. He greeted me by saying, 'I suppose that you are the sort of young man who thinks that Picasso is a better painter than Landseer.' I had to admit that this was so.

Alan Ayckbourn

As a young, promising playwright with all of two West End hits behind me, I was once introduced to the veteran Yorkshire dramatist, J. B. Priestley.

After the introduction, he stared at the young upstart for several seconds. 'You're a very good writer,' he grunted. I smiled gratefully. Then he added, 'So I've heard.'

Sir Richard Dobson

At our wedding reception in 1946 an old RAF friend approached my new mother-in-law and said, 'I am so glad your daughter is marrying Richard, I have known him a long time and he is always at his best in trying circumstances.'

'So I've heard'

John Bratby

On seeing my portrait of him, Bill Frazer said, 'Well, it's certainly a Bratby,' and disappeared.

John Julius Norwich

One of the best compliments I remember was addressed by the former Belgian Ambassador to NATO, André de Staercke, to my mother in respect of an unusually strong cheese which appeared one day on her luncheon table. I still remember him gazing at it, inhaling deeply, closing his eyes and murmuring: 'Ah! ça sent les pieds de Dieu!'

Michael Grade

The moment of truth for any theatrical agent is going backstage to see his or her client on an opening night, after they have performed poorly in a disastrous show. The agent has to spare the client's feelings without making a complete idiot of himself or herself (by this time, the world knows the show's a turkey).

When I was an agent, the technique I used was to embrace the client warmly and exclaim: 'What can I say?' and go on repeating this in the face of the client's cross-questioning.

Others have different techniques, including: 'I don't care what they say, I thought you were terrific', or 'Well, it's all up there on the stage (or screen).'

For the clients who had heard my 'What can I say' routine too often, plan B was: 'Well, you've done it again!'

The agent's lot is not a happy one.

Michael Winner

I was backstage at a Royal Variety Show many years ago when one female actress gushed to another one 'Darling, you were absolutely marvellous'.

To which the other actress replied, 'But I haven't been on yet!'

In the film business one of the terrible moments is when you see a film with the stars or the director and the lights come up at the end, and the film has been absolutely awful and you wonder what to say.

I have coined a few phrases for use in these areas.

To the director you say, 'My gosh, a lot of work went into that'.

To the actor you say, 'My dear chap, you were so *energetic*', or 'I absolutely loved the way you looked.'

There were two very famous bitchy actresses in the past who were doing a film scene, and when you shoot a scene from a film it is important to be in the right place at all times so that you are properly lit in the area the director of photography has placed his lighting.

At the end of this scene actress A said to the other actress:

'Darling, at the end of this scene you are meant to be looking at me.'

To which actress B replied:

'Darling, I am, I am looking at where you are *meant* to be!'

DOUBTFUL
COMPLIMENTS

Lord Murray of Epping Forest

I suppose one of the nicest – unintentional – compliments I ever received in my TUC days was during a demonstration in London. I, foolishly perhaps, got into an argument with a particularly unprepossessing Trotskyite woman whose support we didn't want for our cause. To try to end the conversation I said, 'What you don't see is that there are two sides to this question.' 'That,' she said, poking a bony finger into my chest, 'is just your problem Murray, you think there are two sides to every b— question.'

Sir Harry Secombe

In my early career in show business I spent many frustrating years playing Variety Theatres all over the country, as a second spot comedian. Not the greatest job in the world I must admit! I was leaving the stage door of the Salford Hippodrome after the first house performance when a man in a cloth cap came up to me and said, 'Eeh, you nearly had me laughing when you were on there tonight.' He meant it as a compliment, but it filled me with despair.

'Eeh, you nearly had me laughing . . .'

Paul Eddington

Some years ago I was stopped in the street by a woman who said, 'I saw you in that thing last night – oh, you *were* good! *Oh*, you were good! It's the best thing you've done!'

I reached for my pen.

'You're usually so wooden,' she said.

James Herriot

One back-handed compliment has stuck in my mind over the years. It was back in the forties when, as a young veterinary surgeon in Yorkshire, I was trying to make my way in country practice and desperately anxious to win the esteem of my farmer clients. All vets have places where they can do nothing right – farms where all cases go wrong, even though it is sheer bad luck and nothing to do with the treatment. I was driving into one of my jinx farms and when I got out of the car the farmer looked at me gloomily, obviously dismayed that I and not one of my colleagues was visiting him.

'By gum,' he grunted. 'My wife says it's allus fatal when Mr Herriot walks onto this place.'

I must have looked very downcast, so, being a kindly man, he put a hand on my shoulder and continued, 'Mind you,' he said, 'she likes you as a man.'

Sir Robin Gillett

One of the duties of the Lord Mayor of London was to attend as Guest of Honour at receptions given by the other

Boroughs that comprise Greater London. Towards midnight at a 'knees-up' in Tower Hamlets I thought it time for the Mayoral party to leave, so gathered up my flock to this end. The Toastmaster, who was dancing with one of the entertainers who had sung earlier, spotted my intention, broke off and came over. I explained that we did not wish to disturb the party which was obviously going to continue for some hours but he insisted, 'I must make an announcement, so that the assembled company may applaud your departure.' I knew what he meant, but he might have phrased it differently!

Sir Richard Dobson

After I retired as a Chairman, I wrote to my London bank and asked them to increase my facility for drawing cash from the Richmond branch. The London manager 'phoned me the following morning and said, 'Of course, Sir Richard, you may draw up to £500 a week, bearing in mind who you were – I mean, who you are.'

George the Sixth was shown by John Piper a painting he had done of Windsor Castle in a violent thunderstorm, lots of lurid lights, chiaroscuro etc. The King said, 'Jolly good, old man, but p-pity you had such b-bloody bad luck with the weather.'

Steve Race

I suppose you could call it a compliment in a way! The fact is that I have an absolute hatred of direct mail, junk mail, call it what you will, and object to being put on what I gather the trade calls 'sucker lists'.

So it was that on getting an unsolicited wodge of literature from a Major Somebody-or-other on behalf of a services charity, I wrote to ask that my name and address be removed from his files.

He replied that he would: my name had already been removed. And he added: 'You may be interested to know that we got your name and address from *Who's Who*. Unfortunately we cannot arrange for your name to be removed from that.'

Roger de Grey

When I was Treasurer of the Royal Academy I was awarded by an *independent* jury the major award for a work of distinction in the Summer Exhibition. I was overwhelmed! At the RA banquet the President said: 'We congratulate Roger de Grey for his award . . . he helps us, we help him!'

Sir Frank Layfield QC

In his judgement on an unusually difficult case the judge said, 'Mr Layfield put the plaintiff's contentions with a vigour, clarity, precision and thoroughness which I admired and found helpful and illuminating. As a result I now appreciate the weakness of his argument.'

The Reverend Roger Royal

I was sitting at home one day when the telephone rang. It was someone asking me if I could possibly get down to Paignton to speak at a dinner. I replied that if they could get me there I would certainly go. They made the necessary arrangements. On reaching Paignton there was a gentleman waiting to greet me, looking very smart indeed. It was obvious that someone had let them down and I was standing in at the last minute. I asked the gentleman, 'Who am I standing in for?' 'Diana Dors,' he replied.

STRICTLY
UNCOMPLIMENTARY

Lord Alexander QC

A young barrister, call him Mr Green, was making his first plea in mitigation for a defendant for whom there was not much of obvious merit to be said. He suffered from the nerves which should affect all advocates, but in an acute form, so the exchange went as follows:

'My Lord, my unfortunate client . . .' and he dried up.

He tried a second, and a third time, but on each occasion he got no further than saying, 'My Lord, my unfortunate client . . .'.

At this point, the judge leaned forward with a smile of encouragement and said:

'Go on, Mr Green. So far the Court is in entire agreement with you.'

Kingsley Amis

I was once taken out to dinner at a very expensive restaurant by an old friend who has spent years in the business. Everything about it was wrong – the food, the service and, needless to say, the price. As we left, my friend murmured to the proprietor, who was hanging about in the hope of a compliment, 'How lucky you are to be so successful.' We just had time to see the smile begin to fade from his face as we scooted through the door.

'The Court is in entire agreement with you'

Geoffrey Dear

I was experiencing trouble with my golf swing. All too often it produced a drive of respectable length but with a prodigious hook to the left. The professional advised a change of stance, a change of grip and much practice – alone – on my forthcoming holiday in Scotland.

Thus it was that two weeks later, late one evening – alone – I teed up on a tiny nine hole golf course in Gairloch, Wester Ross. I addressed the ball, swung – and produced the hook!

The ball flew over a low boundary wall alongside the course, struck the tarmac road running parallel to the fairway and with mighty bounds hurtled away from me. It flew over the head of a young man who appeared, hand in hand with his girlfriend, round the corner walking towards me. Without faltering in their steps they walked steadily towards me. I put down another ball, 'played hockey' with it for safety sake up the fairway and, embarrassed, bid them 'Good evening' as we passed, the wall between us.

Walking steadily on and looking straight ahead with a straight face the young man replied quietly, 'If I'd noon ye were going te play golf on the rood I'd have walked on the golf course.'

Game set and match – or whatever the equivalent is in golf!

John Bratby

Donald Pleasance pointing to a large portrait I did of him in his wardrobe, 'I bought your portrait of me so that no one else would be able to see it.'

Admiral
Sir William Staveley

When Her Majesty receives a visiting Head of State she requires, amongst others, the Chiefs of Staff of each of the armed forces to be present. In my full dress uniform I was being driven along the M25 bound for Windsor and the arrival of His Majesty King Olav of Norway when there was a loud bang from the engine of my official car and we came gently to stop, never to move again. Telephoning an SOS on the motorway emergency telephone I sat anxiously awaiting rescue. In the nick of time a police car picked me up and we sped to Windsor.

We arrived only two minutes after the prescribed time. The brightly coloured, lights-flashing police car drew up behind the Royal Pavilion and the Lord Lieutenant greeted me. I suspect I was more relieved than he was! But then one of my colleagues came over and remarked, 'William, I am so glad you have been allowed out on parole!'

Dame Eva Turner

I was singing Santuzza in 'Cavalleria Rusticana' at the Royal Opera House, Covent Garden in one of the International Seasons. I made a special point of rushing to hear Gigli singing the role of Canio in 'Pagliacci', the twin opera, during the rehearsal. It was very special staging with a lovely donkey. The chorus in the opening of 'Pagliacci' is rather difficult and was not going too well. Suddenly the donkey 'performed'. Sir Thomas Beecham who was conducting, put down his baton and announced in these terms, 'Ladies and gentlemen, I see our opinion is reflected above.'

John Francome

The following was said in front of me to Doug Marks (trainer) by F. T. Winter (trainer) after I'd gone to the wrong part of the gallops and as a consequence turned up late. At the time I was still an apprentice.

'They keep telling me he's going to be a good jockey. I don't think he's got the brains to wash cars.'

Erich Segal

After my 'pop' success with 'Love Story', I had some difficulty maintaining my reputation for scholarly *gravitas* in the academic world.

The following incident is but one of many examples.

As I mounted the podium in a distinguished American university to lecture on Greek Tragedy, I noticed that the room seemed rather populated for my esoteric topic. And there appeared to be an inordinate number of teenage girls in the back row.

After the chairman had introduced me, I took a final glance at the young ladies and launched into my lecture, full of sound and fury signifying – I hope – something.

My topic turned truly sombre as I discussed Euripides' attitude towards the atrocities of the Peloponnesian War, dramatically criticized in the 'Trojan Women'. I grew emotional, and hoped my audience did likewise.

A quick glance assured me that the professors in the front row were duly grave. The nymphs at the back, however, had begun to yawn, squirm and chat to one another.

What had I done wrong?

As it happened, the young ladies were right in front of me as we all exited the lecture hall and I heard one complain with irritation: 'He was funnier on the Johnny Carson Show.'

The Right Honourable
Bernard Wetherill

Shortly after I was elected to Parliament in 1964, I moved an Amendment to the Selective Employment Tax (on behalf of tailors and others with work-rooms attached to retail shops) which, to my astonishment, was accepted by the government of the day! I was subsequently summoned by Ian McLeod, the 'Shadow' Chancellor of the Exchequer, who warmly congratulated me, and, as I remember, also asked my name! I replied modestly that I did not presume to speak unless I really knew my subject. I have never forgotten his (kind?) reply, 'Dear boy, I am not certain we shall be hearing you very often!'

The Right Honourable
Sir Michael Palliser

When Disraeli was asked to define the difference between a tragedy and a disaster he replied, 'If Mr Gladstone fell into the Thames and drowned it would be a tragedy, but if he fell in and were pulled out alive it would be a disaster.'

Sir Hugh Casson

Said to me (late in life) at a party, 'Excuse me, weren't you Hugh Casson?'

BOUQUETS

Sir Edward Pickering

One night in 1968 I was catching the 6.50 Waterloo/Portsmouth train which took me to my home in Haslemere. I entered a carriage, sat down and found John Betjeman in the opposite seat. Immediately he launched into a sad story of how he was doing a television series on the life of Tennyson; how he was on his way to Farringford (Tennyson's Isle of Wight home) to record one part of the series; but how he lacked material for the second part dealing with Aldworth (Tennyson's Haslemere home for the last 25 years of his life).

By an astonishing coincidence, I had that week received from Sir Charles Tennyson (Tennyson's grandson and biographer) an essay recalling memories of life at Aldworth with his grandfather. I handed a copy of the essay to Betjeman and thought no more of it, until on 26 September 1968, he wrote me the following letter:

'What I wanted to ask you was whether you knew I was going down to Portsmouth by the 6.50 that evening, when you got out at Haslemere, and I was bound for the Isle of Wight? If you did not know then the coincidence is most extraordinary because of what happened the next day. You will remember that you gave me a very useful essay on Aldworth by Sir Charles, which I was able to make use of, when we filmed the following Friday at Aldworth. But on the next day to that on which I met you, our last shots on the Island after doing Farringford were of Emily Tennyson's tomb in Freshwater Churchyard. The sun shone and the camera was to pan up to the Downs beyond Farringford, after which there was to be a mix into the view from Aldworth. While this was happening I was to read "June bracken and heather" which, as you will remember, was Tennyson's dedication to Emily of his last book of poems. Twice we couldn't take the shot because of noise, once from hovercraft or some such thing, and the other time from aeroplanes. At the third take there was silence enough, and when I came to the bit about the June blue heaven, all the birds around burst into song, as though it were spring, and the cameraman noticed the startled look on my face.

'I ask you the question at the top of the previous paragraph because if our meeting was a true coincidence, it looks as though the Tennysons are watching you and me.'

Barbara Cartland

The nicest compliment I have ever had was after I had been out dancing one night, with a most handsome and charming young man.

When I awoke there was a bouquet of flowers awaiting me with the message:

'Good morning, darling. I want these flowers to see you.'

Dame Cicely Saunders

This is a compliment paid to me when I met a fellow houseman as I came to visit an acquaintance in hospital:

'How nice to see you. If you ever came visiting me with a little bunch of flowers in your hand I should be very alarmed!'

The Right Honourable Christopher Chataway

I was 44 years old. Suddenly it was middle age and felt like it. The lady, who was coming to lunch, seemed a great deal younger.

I was in the greengrocer's, gloomily pondering this divide and picking over the fruit and tomatoes, replacing all those that were mockingly overripe and unappealing.

The shop-keeper appeared – evidently irritated by this fastidious approach to his wares. One could never have guessed at the shining gleaming compliment he was about to deliver with so little grace.

'What do *you* want, young man?'

Within a few months the lady and I were married and lived happily ever after.

Bryan Forbes

I think the most gracious compliment I was ever paid came from a Frenchman. It so happened that many years ago the Directors' Guild of America honoured me with a retrospective, and on the night in question one of my old films – The L-shaped Room – was being shown. Unbeknown to me, the star of the film, Leslie Caron, brought as her guest the great French director Jean Renoir. When the lights went up I was introduced to him for the first time and said how pleased I was to be able to tell him that I had admired him for twenty years. He topped my compliment in a way that I could not possibly emulate. He replied, 'Then we are equal, for I have just admired you for two hours.'

The Very Reverend Alan Webster

Working at St Paul's for ten years leads to every kind of compliment and the reverse. A well-wisher was so pleased with the Prince Charles–Princess Diana wedding that he wrote and suggested that we should all be made Dukes.

Roald Dahl

The famous American actress, Catherine Cornell, once told me how she had first met the man she married who was a stage director. She said that he came up to her without introduction during a cocktail party, held out a bowl of peanuts, looked into her eyes and said, 'I wish they were emeralds'.

Diana Rigg

A Romanian fellow once wrote me a fan letter. The opening paragraph of which read: 'My incestuous thoughts are rushing desirous towards you'.

Martyn Lewis

It is not the critic who counts – not the man who points out how the strong man stumbles, or where the doer of deed could have done better. The credit belongs to the man who is actually in the arena – whose face is marred by dust and sweat and blood – who strives valiantly – who errs and comes short again and again because there is no effort without error and short-coming – who does actually strive to do the deeds – who knows the great enthusiasms, the great devotions, spends himself in a worthy cause – who, at the best knows in the end the triumph of high achievement – and who at the worst, if he fails, at least fails while daring greatly, so that his place shall never be with those cold and timid souls who knew neither victory nor defeat.

Theodore Roosevelt

Sir Alastair Burnet

I have always thought the best literary compliment was paid by David Hume to Adam Smith in a letter of 12 April 1759.

'. . . A wise man's Kingdom is his own Breast: Or, if he looks farther, it will only be to the Judgement of a select few, who are free from Prejudices, & capable of examining his Work. Nothing indeed can be a stronger Presumption of Falshood than the Approbation of the Multitude; and Phocion, you know, always suspected himself of some Blunder, when he was attended with the Applauses of the Populace.

'Supposing, therefore, that you have duely prepard yourself for the worst by all these Reflections; I proceed to tell you the melancholy News, that your Book has been very unfortunate: For the Public seem disposed to applaud it extremely.'

137